LITTLE WITNESS

Aug. 11th, 2016

Dear Anne,
So lovely
to finally meet you.

Connie Roberts

Love,

Connie

LITTLE WITNESS

ARLEN
HOUSE

Little Witness

is published in 2015 by
ARLEN HOUSE
42 Grange Abbey Road
Baldoyle
Dublin 13
Ireland
Phone/Fax: 353 86 8207617
Email: arlenhouse@gmail.com
arlenhouse.blogspot.com

Distributed internationally by
SYRACUSE UNIVERSITY PRESS
621 Skytop Road, Suite 110
Syracuse, NY 13244–5290
Phone: 315–443–5534/Fax: 315–443–5545
Email: supress@syr.edu

978–1–85132–115–5, paperback

Typesetting by Arlen House
Cover image: 'A Head of Steam' by Aidan McDermott
is reproduced courtesy of the artist

Little Witness won the 2013 Listowel Writers' Week Poetry Collection Award, sponsored by Profile Developments, Glin, Co Limerick

CONTENTS

9   Preface

13   Omphalos
14   Not the Delft School
15   Quiet Time
16   Arts and Crafts
17   On Looking into *The Sunday Press* Photo of Convent
     Children Looking into a Stable
19   The Bread Bin was Empty
20   Earliest Memory
21   A Crown for Their Last Night in Ballybrittain
24   Good-For-Nothing Irish Blues
26   (Eden) Derry
27   Inheritance
32   Letterfrack Man
34   The Boys From the Bunkhouse
36   Vignette
37   Little Witness
38   A Winter's Night
39   The Potato Picker and the TV Rental Man
40   Late-night Sport
41   Wounds
44   Litany
45   Altar
46   Rhesus
47   Shoe Shining Day
48   A Modest Proposal
50   Mother Visits the Orphanage
51   Lady Bracknell's Take on Misery Lit
52   Three Sheets
53   Oasis
54   Maisie's Farm
55   The Cupboard

56 Audition
57 The Laundry
58 Holy Angels
59 Molly and Rose
60 Sister Raphael and the Orphan Girl
61 For the Love of God
62 Banister
63 Pallas Lake
64 Seeing
66 Acceptance
67 Shelter
68 Mosaic
70 Lipstick
71 The Screamers
72 Trimble's Bridge
73 Doctor Rabbit
76 Are Yeh There, Missus?
77 Rondeau on Hearing of Your Suicide
78 Sexual Abuse: One
79 I Dreamt I Saw Peter Tyrrell Last Night
81 The Cardigan
83 The Old Woman who Lived in a Shoe
85 Sexual Abuse: Two
86 Transubstantiation
87 At the Algonquin
88 Campground, The Adirondacks

90 *Notes*
94 *Acknowledgements*
96 *About the Author*

For Pete and Aedan

'Keep digging for the good turf'
Seamus Heaney to the author, New York City, 1998

PREFACE

From what I can gather, I was first admitted to Mount Carmel Industrial School, County Westmeath in 1968, at the age of five. In 1971, a younger brother and I were returned to our parents' home in County Offaly. Ten months later, we were transferred back to the orphanage, where I remained until I was seventeen. All of my fourteen siblings spent their childhoods in Irish industrial schools.

The names of certain people mentioned in this collection have been changed for the protection of the individuals concerned.

LITTLE WITNESS

OMPHALOS

No Mossbawn or Inniskeen
to take down from a shelf
and leaf through. No banks of earth
embroidered with ferns and bluebells,
no rabbits running through the thicket,
nor wrens sheltering in the boxwood hedge.

My *omphalos* is a pigeon-grey orphanage yard
clotted with kids: see-saws, pissy knickers,
a clay-filled *Kiwi* tin on a hopscotch square,
British Bulldog, freckled faces, conkers
on shoelaces, pig-tailed girls twirling twine
skipping ropes by St Martha's kitchen,
Jack stones, scabby knees, chinny-alley marbles,
and alongside the cloister, two-seater barn-red swings
we ride like horses till Miss Carberry's *Supper! Supper!*

Galloping from the scullery to the laundry
– my brother riding piggyback – I trip.
Like dripping solder, globules of blood
fall from my nose to the concrete turf.
My baptism? A call to bear witness, brazen.

NOT THE DELFT SCHOOL
for Vonnie McDermott

If I were in a Vermeer or a De Hooch,
I'd rest my head on a mother's lap,
the radiant light from the outdoors
illuminating the spacious, tiled kitchen

as she tenderly searched my hair.
But I am in St Brigid's dormitory –
grey linoleum floor, alb-white candlewick
bed spreads, porcelain sinks – with a dozen

aproned girls and Miss Higgins.
Older girls search younger girls' heads
with fine-tooth combs, stopping every now
and then to squash a louse or nit between

thumb nails. One girl, for fun, shakes
her head over a sink. Scores of wingless
insects, like grains of ground pepper,
cling to the china whiteness.

The housemother douses some heads
with paraffin oil; others get their hair
tied up in green and gold ribbons.
Overhead, a fluorescent light flickers.

QUIET TIME
for Rita

Long after the keys stopped jangling
and the corridor lights were quenched –
after double-checking to see my younger sister
was asleep – I reached, in darkness,
behind the purple velveteen curtains for
my orange. (I'd have bought it with my pocket money
in Jack Galvin's earlier in the day).
Cradled its pockmarked skin slowly in my hands,
inhaled the scent of a Valencia grove before
plunging my thumbnail into its abundant peel.
Pulled it back slowly, like a band-aid from a scraped knee.

As the staff downstairs steeped the grey porridge
for next day's breakfast, I piled the thick rinds
higgledy-piggledy on my chest; licked the piquant
spray from my palms and fingers. Segment by
juicy segment, savoured the succulent fruit
in my mouth. Alone – the council men
digging in the pipes beside my bed,
on a tea-break – in my aromatic orangery.
Next morning: awoke to the smell of
my sister's pissed-in oilskin bed.

ARTS AND CRAFTS

Besides the woollen tea-cozy the portly teapot
never wore, the rag-doll sewn from cast-off

bodices and pinafores, the ice-lolly house
chock-full of crocheted doilies and embroidered

handkerchiefs, the hollow papier-mâché head I carried
under my arm from school, there was the Christmas crib,

where clumps of cotton snow plucked from sanitary
towels – stolen from a locked cupboard

in Our Lady's dorm – absorbed the bitter wind that winter,
protecting the bloody lamb bleating in the manger.

ON LOOKING INTO *THE SUNDAY PRESS* PHOTO OF CONVENT CHILDREN LOOKING INTO A STABLE
Bethlehem, Ireland, Christmas, 1970

I

I see Katie, palms joined, thumbs crossed,
cherub mouth frozen forever in the eternal O
of *Gloria in Excelsis Deo*. Helen, in faux-fur
collared mini-coat, bespectacled head cocked sideways
like a dog, hands clasped like an old man,
agog at the wax infant in the winter straw.
Joseph, ears sticking out, spic and span
in short-pants communion suit. Nutcracker straight.
Innocent, head-banded Maureen, a world away
from the beatings, self-mutilation, murder.
A nun rests her hands on Mary and Brendan.
Tony, never one to follow rules, looks away.
And I, in patent leather shoes and white knee socks,
thumbs hooked in woollen coat pockets – no stranger to
straw and barns – stand nonchalant.

II

Did our neighbours know we sneaked
into their barn at night?
That mother covered us in coats
as we slept on their bales of straw?
Did they think the farm dog
barked at a midnight stranger
going to the community pump
for water? Did they know
we, furtive as field mice, looked
across the hedges for the light
that said he was home? That our eyes
penetrated the God-forsaken fields
and saw his murderous rage?
That in the stillness, we could still
hear the borrowed dishes crashing
to the flagstone floor?

Did they know mother roused us
before they awoke, shepherding us
home to our bloody pen?

THE BREAD BIN WAS EMPTY

I

The bread bin was empty, the money
   gone. What was she supposed to do
to feed her babies? Beg? Not likely.
   The bread bin was empty, the money
gone on Guinness for himself, free
   rounds for the lads. Of course he knew
the bread bin was empty, the money
   gone, but what was he supposed to do?

II

The Lord helps those who help themselves.
   My mother took Him at His word.
We stole into the church like elves.
   The Lord helps those who help themselves,
so into the poor-box we delved
   and robbed its contents unperturbed.
The Lord helps those who help themselves,
   and mother took Him at His word.

EARLIEST MEMORY

High up in the air in the arms of
a garda, his fire-lit buttons as shiny
as gold foil on chocolate coins.

Night, way past my bedtime.
He asks if I saw Daddy hit Mammy.
I drag my eyes from his kind face

to my mother's desperate blue eyes,
from there to my father's baleful stare,
back to the face a few inches from mine, and lie.

A CROWN FOR THEIR LAST NIGHT IN BALLYBRITTAIN
for Tony

As they rounded Conroy's corner from school,
they sensed something was awry: the squat house
– dark, silent – sat on its haunches, its spool
of smoke missing. He'd gone to town ravenous
for drink. They sat with their mother, the clock
ticking loudly on the dresser, afraid
to ask, *when's Daddy coming home?* The look
on her face said it all. Soon he'd parade
through the door, his face black, bloated. Bulbous
eyes, red as the blood that ran down his face
(he'd have fallen off his bike). Murderous
intentions. Sweeping brush in hand, he'd chase
the kids out into the fields. They'd hear her
squeal, *no, Bob, no!* as they ran like terriers.

We heard her squeal, but ran like terriers
down the yard, past the turf stack, under barbed
wire to the long grass. Crouched there like curs
in a ditch till we got cold. I whispered
to my brother, *Let's say the rosary
for Mam. Our Father who art in heaven …*
But our prayers couldn't drown the war
inside the house: dishes in smithereens;
you fuckin' bitch, I'm going to kill you!
Then Old Spollen passed by driving his cattle
home: *I'd help, if I knew what to do.*
God knows, it's none of my business, a leanbh.
He crossed himself, then cracked his ash-plant on
a cow's broad back. Stared straight ahead; was gone.

We stared straight ahead like cows at the house,
waiting for the battle to end. It spilled
out into the yard. Bleeding from the mouth
and head, she tried to run, but he pummelled

her harder. She fell, the coarse gravel
kissing her face. When he hit her with a rock,
her low moans mingled with the caramel
evening, like one of Old Spollen's livestock.
He soon grew tired when she refused to budge;
shouted at our silhouettes in the field,
yeh pair-a-bastards, come here! My brother peed
in his short pants. As the urine trickled
into his wellies, our mother crawled
inside the house. Father stared, his eyes crow-black.

His eyes, crow-black, bored into us as we
squirmed under the barbed wire like rats
under a barn door. Hearts hammering in our ears,
we smelt his rage, tasted his terror. He spat
a phlegmy spit into the ditch and smiled.
That's it … come to Daddy. A corncrake *crrek crrek-ed*
in the distance. Father tucked his shirt in, styled
his hair with a comb. Cock of the meadow,
he strode toward the door. *Yer mother's had a bit
of an accident … she fell off a chair.*
Blood splattered the walls and floor; opposite
the St Anthony picture, a blade
knifed the layers of smoke-sooted wallpaper.
Mam, her back to us, cowered in the corner.

Her back to us, Mam cowered in the corner
of the kitchen like a beaten hound beneath
a table. Willow-patterned plates, a canister
of tea, cutlery lay scattered at her feet.
Afterwards, my father liked to have a steak
(that he'd bring from town) and a cigarette.
He told her to cook it well, with *a rake
of onions,* that he'd be back in a minute,
he was just going to Winston's for fags.
Would I like to go along? On the crossbar
of the bike, his soured Guinness breath flooded

my nostrils as he cycled this way and that
up the road. I caught my foot in the spokes;
we landed in the ditch before he got his smokes.

In the feckin' ditch we landed before I
got me smokes! Christ, what did Mrs Winston
think at all? Woman, where's my fuckin' fry?
The smell of beef and bitter-sweet onions
made my mouth water. Father ate alone.
What the hell are you limpin' for? Walk straight!
My foot swelled like blown glass on the stone floor.
In the stifling hot kitchen we waited,
my mother and I. (She hid Tony in
the back room, his blond head covered in coats).
I fetched the pink plastic bucket, and within
15 minutes, right on cue, he vomited.
My mother looked at the curdled brown mess
and saw the supper her children didn't get.

My children didn't get supper that night,
but sure, that was nothing new. Off to school
they'd often go without a bite, despite
my best efforts. A suffering eejit, a fool,
that's all I was. Oh, 'tis well I recall
their last night in Ballybrittain. How my child
sneaked out of her father's bed – an animal
gnawing itself from a snare. My little red
fox dragging her paw across the cold floor,
out to the acrid kitchen where I lay in
a shambles by the hearth. Only God knows
the part of me that died that night as she cleansed
the dried blood from my wounds and spoon-fed me tea.
Next day, the nuns took them away from me.

GOOD-FOR-NOTHING IRISH BLUES

The ould fella came home fluthered again last night.
Yeh hear me?
The ould fella came home fluthered again last night.
He'd fallen off his bike and was in the mood for a fight.

Didn't like the steak I cooked.
Said it was like shoe leather.
Didn't like the feckin' steak I cooked.
Said it was tough as leather.
Hit me with the frying pan.
Didn't wait for it to cool neither.

Years he's punished me with his fists.
Kicked me in the groin.
Years he's punished me with his fists.
Kicked me in the groin.
Whisht, once he tried to drown me in the Grand Canal.

The judge said he'd always be a good-for-nothing
way back when.
Aye, the judge said he'd always be a wastrel
way back when.
But that judge don't see how hard he tries
time and time again.

Had 15 children with this man.
All of them reared by the State.
Jaysus, 15 young wans with this man.
All of them reared by the State.
June we'll be married 50 years.
Sure that's something to celebrate.

Betimes I pretend I'm crazy.
Check into the mental home.

Betimes I pretend I'm crazy.
Check into the mental home.
But I'm no sooner there than I'm thinking
of the quare fella all alone.

The ould fella came home fluthered again last night.
Yeh hear me?
The ould fella came home fluthered again last night.
He'd fallen off his bike and was in the mood for a fight.

(Eden) Derry

Never as exotic as the time I was transferred from
home back to the orphanage mid-term.

Sr Johanna's class, 1971 – Nana Mouskouri's
'till the white rose blooms again' playing

on the record player – a town girl, brave enough
to approach me, whispered, *So, where are you from?*

Edenderry, I whispered back.
Derry, where The Troubles are?

It might have been the way she sidled a little closer
to me, or maybe it was the grainy, black and white images

of balaclavaed youths hurtling petrol bombs
at armoured cars that made me answer,

Aye, Derry, where the troubles are.

INHERITANCE

in memory of the Poor Clare Orphanage fire, 23 February 1943, Cavan

I

It would be easy to saccharine their deaths
with morning dew (God knows, it could happen
to a bishop, or a poet). But I won't sing
of winged angels and burnished gold;
I won't tell it slant – come, let the blazing truth blind.

II

Hard of hearing, Dolly Duffy slept through
Miss O'Reilly's order to rise and go into
St Clare's, townsmen with axes battering
down the front door, Mary Caffrey's clanging keys,
John McNally's *get the children out!*
Get everyone out! For God's sake, get them out!
the Cassidy Sisters' *Mona! Mona,*
where are you? Over here, Josie, over here!
Sr Felix's *try to put the fire out,*
like a good lad. And the unidentified voice
to the male intruders, *go back down!*
Do you hear me, go back down!
But Una Smith scrambled back up in the heat
and the dark to the Sacred Heart, fingered a rosary
of bed knobs till she found her. Rushing the
Act of Contrition, Dolly placed her apron
on her head like a mantilla and braved
the choking smoke down the wooden stairs.
The last child to exit this way, her soles
smoldering when she stumbled out onto Main Street.

III

Maggie Smith came home (her best years spent
as a live-in skivvy for a doctor or a judge?).
Sure, where else would she go – the Magdalene Laundry?

The County Home? Hadn't St Joseph's been home
since it opened its doors over threescore years before.
Yes, Maggie Smith came home, to the early-morning

prayers in the coffin-cold chapel and the late-night crying
of babies in their cots. Not quite on equal footing
with the nuns but a rung above their charges.

Shawled and shuffling, up the town for bits and bobs –
a bar of *Sunlight* soap or a jar of *Bovril*.
Maggie Smith came home, came home to die.

Ashen-faced, the aged woman hobbled into
St Clare's. As an older girl led the younger ones
in a decade of the rosary, Maggie lay down

on an empty bed – a pyre of striped ticking – and waited.

IV

The lights went dead. Screams now pierced
the choking blackness. *Get us out – we're smothering!*
Sisters called to one another; others crawled on
their bellies to the high windows. Sooty faces

pressed against windowpanes. A girl on her knees
coughed out prayers. And the polished floor
buckled, wardrobes and cots demolished
by famished flames. Timbers crashed, glass smashed

forty feet to the street below. Five little forms
huddled against the dormitory door.
Myth be damned at the sight of the clothes burning
on the back of four-year-old Lizzie Heaphy from Swords.

V

What can be said, the Keystone Brigade bungled
attempts at rescue. Hoses leaked, ladders
couldn't reach, and the *sort-of-but-not-really*
Captain said it took forty-five minutes to
assemble a crew, five minutes more than
it took the fire to swallow thirty-five children
and one old woman. Tell me, how does that add up?

VI

But that pre-Lenten night Cavan, like any Irish town,
had its blessings too. Men beckoned children

on hot windowsills to jump into their outstretched arms.
Veronica took a leap of faith. Maureen slipped

through one man's embrace breaking her legs.
Another fell on a lean-to shed.

An ESB ladder was procured and hoisted,
a GAA man and a doctor risked life and limb

to reach the smoke-billowing windows,
before the heavens came crashing down.

VII

36 bodies,
eight coffins, Cullies graveyard.
No memorial.

VIII

Children of the Poor Clares,
pray for us.
The 13 Marys
have mercy on us.

Mary Barrett
Mary Brady
Mary Carroll

Mary Galligan
Mary Harrison
Mary Hughes

Mary Ivers
Mary Kelly
Mary Lowry

Mary Lynch
Mary Roche
Mary O'Hara

Mary McKiernan

Children of the church
children most pure
children most vulnerable

Kathleen Chambers
Kathleen Kiely
Kathleen Reilly

Josephine Carroll
Josephine Cassidy
Mona Cassidy

Ellen Morgan
Ellen Payne
Harriet Payne

Nora Barrett
Margaret Chambers
Dorothy Daly

Frances Kiely
Bridget Galligan
Susan McKiernan

Elizabeth Heaphy
Ellen McHugh
Philomena Regan

Bernadette Serridge
Margaret Lynch
Teresa White

Rose Wright

Pray for us, o children of God.
Pray that our indifference will
not be our inheritance.

LETTERFRACK MAN
after Seamus Heaney's *The Tollund Man*
i.m. Peter Tyrrell (1916–1967)

I

One day I will go to Hampstead Heath
to read his postscript, written in
oily black ash that Friday in April.
In that hollowed ground
where they found him,
his last meal, a pint and a take-away,
burnt offerings,
his overcoat melted to the bone,
I will stand a long time;
weep that it took so long for his
match to spark a revolution.

II

By God, I'll risk blasphemy.
Beatify this blessed boy from Letterfrack.

Ask him to intercede on behalf of the mother
on the pub-stool draining the dregs of her

redress cheque, the bed-sit-bound bachelor,
his meds cocktail barely keeping his demons

at bay. Ask him to pray for the put away
and the put-together, for those who wear their scars

in the media or in their hearts, for the broke
and the broken, the prisoner and the politician.

God knows, it's a miracle they survived at all.

III

Something of his sad escape
– unflinching in the flame –
comes to me as the TV blasts

news of a fruit-and-veg vendor
a continent away:
whispering the names

Goldenbridge, Ferryhouse, Artane,
watching the uplifted fists,
the batons and the burning tyres,

I feel at sea, unmoored and moored.

THE BOYS FROM THE BUNKHOUSE
for Dan Barry

The turkey plant case has really haunted all of us.
This is what happens when we don't pay attention.
Curt Decker, Executive Director, National Disability Rights Network

The boys from the bunkhouse are shackling toms
in a heartland turkey processing plant.
It happens when we don't pay attention.

Roused by the boss man each day at 3am
– plucked from their dreams of pulling guts – hadn't
the boys from the bunkhouse just been shackling toms?

Hang those doggone turkeys, boy, hang 'em, hang 'em,
and another punch from the on-site tyrant.
It happens when we don't pay attention.

Pulling crop for the pop and the Honey Bun
at the Atalissa Mini Mart,
the boys from the bunkhouse keep shackling toms.

It sticks in Alford Busby's craw. He hobbles
toward winter fields, white as feathers; screams, *I ain't* ...
Men die in ditches when we don't pay attention.

Willie Levi, the turkey husher, calms
the frightened fowl – *ok, tom, quiet down* –
while the boys from the bunkhouse keep shackling toms.

Wings clipped, they've worked the inverted, fettered
birds for 30 years without decent pay.
God help us for not paying attention.

Back in the bunkhouse with its mould and vermin,
they make calls to numbers long off the hook,
the boys from the Lone Star State who shackle toms.

There comes a time to put the turkeys down,
the pinners, the croppers and the rehangers.
Finally, someone who pays attention.

Millions in damages brings some redemption,
but the Penner brothers are content to be
away from the bunkhouse and the shackled toms.

And Willie Levi likes to get his dance on
with his girlfriend, Rose, on their weekly date.
Good riddance to the bunkhouse and the shackled toms:
It can happen ... if we pay attention.

VIGNETTE

Their cows milked, two ruddy-faced farmers
lean over a five-bar field gate. My father passes
on his bicycle. *I'm off to mass, boys!*
says he to them. *Isn't he a great fellow*
the way he goes to mass every morning? says one
to the other. *Well, Seamus,* says the other back,
if he was to ate 50 pounds of the marble altar
beyond in that church, he's still going to hell!

LITTLE WITNESS

To stop it from crying,
my father picks up the bare-bottomed

baby from its cot, holds it
upside-down by the ankles,

like a plucked turkey,
and beats the stuffing out of it.

A Winter's Night

A child sits on her mother's knee
in the hot kitchen, silently

listening for the gate's wrought-iron
yelp announcing her father is home.

A skittish mouse scratches the turf box
as the mother mouths to the crucifix

on the wall. Snow powders the dun-brown bog,
like sieved icing sugar on a yule-log.

Cur and cat lie snug in their straw-strewn
kennels. There'll be a dull thud soon,

and the child in bare feet and nightie
– sleet, sharp as pine needles, pricking

her warm face – will struggle to lift
her father out of the torch-lit snowdrift.

She'll prop him in a chair by the fire,
wipe beads from his brow and stroke his hair.

THE POTATO PICKER AND THE TV RENTAL MAN

The purple evening creeping in around him,
frost not far off, legs straddling the drills,
he stoops, like one of Millet's gleaners,
to pick the last of the late potatoes.
If he hears the motor car pull up on
the verge of the vetch-tendriled ditch, he doesn't
lift his head. Inside the house, two children,
seated on Formica chairs, stare at the black and white
western – gun-smoke and dust-clouds circling
the wagons – the rabbit ears set at ten past ten.

As the soft-shoed man struggles to open
the wrought-iron gate with the obstinate television,
before stowing it in the boot, the potato-picker,
his head hanging between his arms like a pendulum,
keeps picking, picking, picking. Hands as big as shovels,
he cradles each potato, gently scrapes the earth
from its cold stoniness, before placing it in a burlap sack.
Tomorrow, he'll dig a pit and store his harvest
in layer after layer of warm straw; come winter,
feast on a bounty of boxty, colcannon and champ.

LATE-NIGHT SPORT

Ok, son, let's have some fun.
That's my boy, pick up your gun.

We'll pretend we're the IRA
and shoot any Brit who gets in our way.

Let's say one comes to our door
tonight, what will you do before

you kill him? Don't be such a sissy,
give the gun to your sister. She

knows how to shoot a *Sassenach* dead.
That's it girl, aim for his head.

Remember, I wore the uniform of those dogs
after the war, but now they're in the bogs

of Ireland where all is fair game.
What are you crying for, you lame

excuse of a boy? Take that
you coward, you sniffling brat.

Now look what you've made me do,
your stupid head broke the gun in two.

Well, the game's over, I'm off to bed,
Tiocfaidh ár lá, as the Fenian said.

WOUNDS

I

He could nurse an injured bird
in a shoe-box or scald a mouse

with a cauldron of boiling water.
He could plant rows of potatoes –

rose-skinned Roosters, deep-eyed Kerrs Pinks –
or fling his dinner to the floor

if the cabbage wasn't to his liking.
He could prune the parish priest's hedges

with a shears, or with a bicycle-pump,
pump Fairy Liquid up into his wife.

II

It's you,
you're why I am
the way I am,
ambushing me
with your red lips,
your basket of eggs
by the banks of the Figile.
I was there to milk cows,
to cut hay,
not to spend my days in a council house
in the arse-hole of Ireland.
God forgive you.
I could've joined the guards
like my father,
settled in the barracks.
Bollix, I could've been McGahern.

Write, right?
You've seen my copy-books.
A great fist at
turning a phrase.
Instead, I turn turf,
potato drills,
silage for fat cows,
plough,
kowtow.
My mother had you pegged.
Dirty? She wouldn't know
the water in the Shannon.
Holy God, so help me
but I'll sluice the filth out of you.
Mother most pure.
Mother most chaste.
Mother undefiled.
Mother of Christ,
your mother
following me home to Tipperary,
forcing me to marry you,
my first son
dead in your belly.
Dusk
I carried him
to the graveyard in Cloncrane,
heard, still hear,
his wooden body
shifting in his
cardboard casket,
a pebble in a match-box,
no priest,
no 'glory be'.
Lord have mercy.
Christ have mercy.
Lord have mercy.
Sweet heart of Jesus

I've a good mind to crucify you,
you shoved my children into
the Cruelty Man's car,
read the *Tribune*,
'tis me nerves, you know, Inspector,
pried them from my arms,
hid them behind thick grey walls,
any wonder I drink
my own flesh and blood.
Body of Christ, save me.
Blood of Christ, inebriate me.
Hide me within your wounds.

LITANY

Take your rosaries, your scapulars, your novenas,
your miraculous medals, your statues, your bible,
your bottle of Lourdes' holy water, your confessions

and absolutions and build a bonfire out of them.
Dear father, let the black, holy smoke rise to the heights
of heaven, let it seep slowly through celestial floorboards,

creep lightly through open windows and choke
all your heavenly mentors. They are nothing
but conspirators in your swath of destruction.

Where was St Anthony when your quarry lay trapped
like a coursing hare underneath your dog's body?
Was St Peter checking *Curricula Vitae* at the gates

when you kicked our mother on the kitchen floor?
No doubt, St Francis was in the divine aviary tending his
sister-birds while you mocked my little brother.

St Patrick, your namesake – was he resting on his shamrocks
as you smashed the willow-patterned plates and burned
our schoolbooks in the open fire? Just how hopeless

did we have to be for St Jude to come to our aid?
Tell your high priests I've gained strength from their
apathy: like a falcon, I fly strong and hard into the wind.

ALTAR

We knew we were Other: our label,
convent children. Sundays we walked
through the town like a herd of goats,
farmer-nun goading us on: *No dilly-dallying*
... step lively ... weekly constitutional.

Miss Cassidy, the maths teacher, promised
a prize to anyone who hadn't missed
a day from school. A lone hand rose in the air.
Convent children don't count – the nuns
make sure ye get to school, sniffles or not.

May, Our Lady's month, town-girls bring flowers
from their mothers' gardens to school.
The nun arranges pink and red blooms
perfectly on the altar. *Stand up, Fidelma.*
Ciúnas, everyone! Take a bow, Lorna.

Back in a room in the orphanage,
on a windowsill behind a curtain,
there's another altar: a mother in blue,
a jam jar full of whispering wild flowers
– bluebells, buttercups, primroses, cowslips.

RHESUS
for Frank Feery

Drooping geraniums we drank him in,
parched for years in our terracotta pots.
He didn't dress in Roy Orbison black,
strum the guitar and sing *Pretty Woman*
in the Far Fields (in his underwear),
like one Raybanned housefather.
Instead, he doled out Cadbury bars for
Quiz Around the Clock; choreographed
Camptown Ladies and *Captain Kelly's Kitchen*
for the orphanage variety show. And one night,
when I awoke sobbing from a nightmare –
my drunken father chasing me through a hedge maze –
he hugged me. Like a rhesus monkey I clung
to him, nuzzling his warm terrycloth frame.

SHOE SHINING DAY
i.m. Miss Winifred Carberry

After the milky tea, poured from the pot-bellied
teapot, was drunk, the crusty sliced pan
and strawberry jam eaten, and the delph washed,
girls jostled their way to the numbered *cassies*
in the long, narrow corridor. Donned aprons –

black-ink names on white bias binding stitched inside –
and fetched their shoes for polishing.
Miss Carberry sat on her wooden throne
in the blue-tiled hallway, her nylon housecoat
– festooned with safety pins and sewing needles,

handkerchiefs and crochet hooks, *Singer* bobbins
and *bainin* yarn – bursting at the bosom.
Her wide-eyed subjects, brushes and rags in hand,
hunkered at her feet, their scuffed brogues neatly
before them. Her lower lip extended, huffing air up

her nostrils, Queen Winnie applied the wax in gusts.
Girls worked their elbows like fiddlers at a *Comhaltas* ceili
till their shoes shone like a parquet floor, stopping every
now and then to peek at the candy-floss-pink bloomers
that courted gartered stockings above thick knees.

A Modest Proposal

From Sr Mary Concepta, Resident Manager,
Mount Carmel Industrial School

And what about love you ask?
Hmm, can't say the thought ever crossed
my mind. You know our task
here is enormous. Don't want to boast,

but have you ever seen a more
well-fed, well-dressed bunch? Well,
well, have you? But I'm not one to ignore
the needs of the children. Do tell

if I don't have the answer
to your question about love?
Now, I'm sure that you'll concur
that nothing speaks more of love than a dog.

Yes, a dog! A furry friend, a pet.
I propose that each nun in the convent
pick a child from the yard to dote
on, as one would do a pet. Hush, no argument!

Children would make terrific dogs. Well,
to be precise, pups. Sr Benedict
is partial to a mongrel terrier.
Sean O'Brien and she, I think, would click.

Sr Aloysious is a fusspot –
she'd want more of a pedigree.
Florrie McCann would make a grand lap dog,
sit quietly as Sister watched TV.

Reverend Mother could have a Jack Russell.
She could take him to the priests' house for tea,

provided, of course, he didn't smell
or shed hair on the Monsignor's settee.

Each pet would have a collar and leash,
with a nametag around its neck.
Nuns could take their dogs to mass, if they please.
They could howl in the choir, what the heck!

They could groom the poor creatures; put their hair
up in bows. Feed them treats from their pockets,
and walk them down Main Street on Sundays. Share
a love that's unique to owners and pets.

As Mother McAuley ministered to the poor,
her Sisters can carry on her good deeds:
through their love and attention, the nuns will ensure
they meet more than the children's physical needs.

Would you like to come home and live with us again, pet?
No, Ma, I'm grand here.

Your father would be very happy.
You know you're his favourite.
No, Ma, honest, I'm grand here.

He really misses you.
He cries at night by the fire.
I'll write letters to him, Ma.

He'll give up the drink if you come home.
Sure, amn't I grand here, Ma.

Please, child, he'll stop beating me if you come home.
I'm sorry, Ma.

If he kills me, I'll come back and haunt you.

LADY BRACKNELL'S TAKE ON MISERY LIT

To suffer one peck of adversity
in childhood may be regarded as
a misfortune, but to suffer bushels
strikes me as misery loves company.

THREE SHEETS

I

Negotiatin' that bridge on a bicycle
is difficult enough if yer sober,
but when yer three sheets to the wind,
'tis well-nigh impossible. Normally, I get off
the bike and walk. But this day, I stayed on.
Sailed right into the Grand Canal, bike first.
A neighbour fished me out. Straight back in I went,
bulrushes and reeds up to me oxters. I mean,
we're talkin' six bottles of Guinness here.
I couldn't just leave them there. You know what
them fish are like for drinkin'.

II

I wrote letters to Daddy
from the orphanage, begging him
not to beat Mammy, to stay off
the drink. Once, I sent him a lock
of my straw-coloured hair.

He wrote letters back to me
in the orphanage, vowing
not to beat Mammy, promising
to take the 'pledge'. Once, he wrote it
on a Guinness bar mat.

III

Christmas Eve, father,
child (and panda bear) bike home
in the falling snow.

OASIS
for foster mother Eileen Sheerin

Back when the collar and the wimple were law,
when you didn't cross the cassock or the habit,
she stood her ground. When she'd meet the Cheshire-cat
nun in town, she'd *nod-nod-nod*, then carry on
about her business – put down a few pounds
on that grand set of china in Joe Feeley's,
pick up an extra roll of wallpaper
for the end room or a few balls of wool
for that Aran jumper. When the Head Nun
wanted to send me, in my 14th year, to the doctor's
house in Kilbeggan, to house-keep, she told her
she had work around her own house – *oh, I've windows to
wash, walls to paint, Sister.*

But devil a window I washed that summer, my sun-soused
days spent traipsing out the Swimming Pool Road
– towel and togs under my arm – my two-and-a-half pence
tucked in my pocket, plus a little extra for the requisite
cream bun in The Oasis on the way home.

When the Head Nun again wanted to dispatch me
(despite my protestations) to my parents' home,
she assured her she'd deliver me – *oh, I'll drive her myself,
Sister, after our holiday in Butlin's Mosney.*

Not a bit of her – she kept me under her red coat, in her
chalet, by the boating lake and the sunken gardens.
And when I aged out of the orphanage and was released
into her care – warned, mind you, not to *sponge off* her
generosity, to soak up my secretarial studies (be a quick
brown fox, not a lazy dog) – she did what any good
mother would do when her pup is hurt by word or world:
put her foot on the clutch, shifted gears, pulled over to the
side of a quiet road.

MAISIE'S FARM
i.m. foster parents Mr and Mrs Coady

Maisie's mother   meets us at the top
of the boreen, bright   and bouncy in her floral
housecoat *hello*   *how was school?*
she gushes her gait   turning into a gallop
buxom breasts   blindly envelop
the dog dances   in the yard delighted,
the white-washed   walls of the cottage
shimmer in the sunlight   smoke billows
from the chimney a charmed   cat chases chickens
her father furrows   the fields with a horse
he waves not wanting   to waste daylight
later we'll all laugh   loudly over dinner
our bellies bulging   from bacon and cabbage
then Maisie and me   will masquerade as tramps
in worn-out worsted   britches and wellingtons
the adults will applaud   and appeal for more
Uncle Pachie will propose   a poem or two
before bed we'll use beads   to belt out the rosary
we'll ask God to be good   to the gaggling geese
not forgetting the frolicsome   lambs or the forlorn sheep
the cud-chewing cows   or the curious goats
nonetheless for now   nothing will suffice
but to swing on the swing   on this swollen evening.

THE CUPBOARD

In the linoleumed corridor, next
to the *cassies,* which held our polished shoes
and aprons, it vanished into the wainscot
panelling. But we knew where it was.
Whose toy hadn't been confiscated and stored
there for safe-keeping after a visit
with a family – my Lucille Ball doll,
with her red-bouffant curls and mischievous smile,
shelved for years, her unblinking blue eyes
twinkling as a caul of cobwebs crept across
her alabaster face, mildew spoiling
her crepe, polka-dot poodle-skirt.
Teddies and tin soldiers met the same fate;
golliwogs and rag-dolls lay in wait.

AUDITION
for Irina O'Gara

She's a veritable Madame Alexander doll
in her ruffled tulle, pink-champagne party dress.
How she skips and sings for the videographer –
she's an indomitable Madame Alexander doll.
She'll be speaking English in no time at all;
day by day, will think of the orphanage less.
Will become an inevitable Barbie doll,
in her fairytale princess gown and clutch purse.

THE LAUNDRY

Great, whirring washing machines. An electric horse –
Trojan-big – *click-clicks* as clothes dry on rows
of wooden pegs. Hissing steam and slurping sluice.
Deep square sinks, with grey-ribbed washboards.

In the Folding Room to the left, a nun feeds
white sheets through a cylindrical mangle;
two flush-faced girls fold the hot, pressed cotton,
dancing back and forth, as in *The Walls of Limerick.*

Friday evening, children with towels rolled
under their arms queue outside a cubicle
for a bath, the wet ceramic tile cold
on their feet, the air headily carbolic.

Though the wooden tables have long been scoured,
the enamel jugs and basins in some antique shop,
out by the clothesline, still, a gaggle of girls,
smoking and laughing, leaning on their mops.

HOLY ANGELS

Where the babies slept:
mottled white steel cots

lined up like infantries.
Soiled nappies steeping

in green and red buckets.
A young girl bottle-feeds a baby;

puts it down for the night.
Next day, whispers to her friend

in school how it never woke up.

MOLLY AND ROSE

I

Big-boned, pale-faced Molly, mouth twisted,
hand lifted like a dog's paw, dragging her
steel-bound leg in her black, laced-up boot,
hobbles across the dormitory, mumbling
wanna smell my hand? Wanna smell my hand?
before clocking you in the head with a fist.

II

She liked creepy-crawlies our Rose Plover,
so much so she ate them, God love her.

Caterpillars it seemed she liked best.
From the convent cabbages, she plucked this pest

and squashed it between her fingers.
Looking down her nose at amateurs,

she promptly swallowed the snot-green goo
and shouted, *come on, I dare yeh!*

SISTER RAPHAEL AND THE ORPHAN GIRL

The only nun in the Civil Defence
first aid class that winter. Born for it, she taught
Irish to reluctant schoolgirls. Intense
and fluent in the classroom, she was fraught
with *imní* among the citizens of the town.
Would a former student snicker when she did
CPR on the dummy? Would a man groan
to find himself a partner with – God forbid –
a bride of Christ? Long evenings in her cell
they bandaged broken bones and sprained ankles.
Once, she removed her veil. Unashamed
of her balding crown, she allowed the girl to dress
her head. Outside, the chapel bells summoned
as the orphan embalmed her mummy-nun.

Stand still! she shouts, twisting the nylons
tighter around my freshly-washed hair.
Her roan mane sits in a modest bun
inches from her crooked spine. A mare
with no foals of her own, but mother
to scores of abandoned, abused – standard
issue industrial school. Because of her,
girls in golden and charcoal ringlets, dresses blanched,
will glide down the aisle in their communion plumage.
Mute swans will bugle to one another lakeside,
nightmares and bed-wetting having migrated south
for a day. Years from now, in the nuns' graveyard,
glutted with rows of white crosses, I'll stand still
among the purple and gold blooms of April.

BANISTER
i.m. Mary Raftery

Oh, give me a little girl
happy to rise to the occasion

and a smiling father
who waits with open arms

at the bottom of the stairs
to catch, to catch, to catch her,

and I'll give you a woman
solid as a granite banister,

with the nerve to change a nation.

PALLAS LAKE
for David

I could have lived the rest of my life in that Sunday,
a John Hinde sky painted on a stone bowl of stilled water,

a phalanx of starlings flitting in and out of
a marquee of greenery, the Kerry Blue chasing

a thrown stick in the rush-mired marsh,
my espadrilles and his steel-toe brogues side by side

on the blanket; in the wicker basket,
brown-bread turkey sandwiches growing warm,

a thermos of tea, cold. If there was a fisherman
in thigh-high waders and camouflage hat trying

to lasso a rainbow trout, we didn't see him.

SEEING

I

Wobbly as I was on a bicycle,
I preferred to thumb a lift out the road
to her white pebble-dashed farmhouse.
The backdoor unlatched, I'd let myself in
and find her by the range – legs akimbo,
nylon stockings rolled down to her ample ankles –
kneading early-morning, back-doorstep slugs
into arthritic knees. The laughs of this old wife
as I told her, job or no job, there was no
way I was going to lay a finger on
any black, gelatinous *shellagopukka*.

Trying to cobble together the airfare
back to America, I packed the months
I spent as a companion to this no-nonsense
myopic woman and carried them across
the sea, up skyscrapers and down brownstones.
Hours reading the local newspapers to her
after our mid-day dinner and *Harbour Hotel*.
Summer afternoons sitting on hard kitchen chairs
in the farmyard, watching the sun melt into
bereft barns and byres, glad of the postman's *tick tick tick*.

II

Visibly shaken each time, my mother
would recount my temporary blindness,
how during a drunken rampage, my father
switched his attention from her to the screeching
toddler in the room, punishing its head on
the flagstone floor, how it went silent, turned purple.

III

When colouring inside the lines is not your
thing, the optometrist's assistant said,
when you want some extra personality,
because who doesn't like extra? When you need
to create a sassy sophistication from day
to night, you must try these feather-light,
fun and funky, beautifully sculpted,
luxurious Italian, cardinal-red
TR90 memory plastic reading glasses
which feature spring hinges, high quality
aspheric lenses and a comfortable
nose-pad for added support. Comes with a
matching, flip-top, clam-shell protective case.

ACCEPTANCE

When the nun took us for our Sunday walk
out the Old Bog Road, I'd lag behind
or sprint ahead, not wanting to be branded

an orphan. When the red and white Volkswagen bus
pulled up outside my foster parents' house
I refused to get in with the other children.

But when the orphanage was razed in the 1990s,
I returned with my American husband;
had tea and rhubarb tart in the aging nuns' parlour.

As we gossiped about Bill and Monica,
my damp palm pawed a brown two-inch tile
salvaged from the contractor's wrecking ball.

SHELTER
after Elizabeth Bishop

Poor bitch, you didn't have a chance, did you?
Dumped in a cardboard box on 10th Avenue.
Where your mother was, nobody knew.

Sleeping under the bridge by the river?
Or strolling Central Park like a tourist,
with a hot dog and Nikon Coolpix?

Now you call a Bowery shelter home,
an ASPCA tag – warm and worn –
swings on your neck like a medal from Lourdes.

How's that pit-bull to your left? I see his wound
has knotted to a scar. And that Basset hound,
still howling like a loon on a Vermont pond?

Christ! You've got to get out of here. It reeks
of a Blarney Stone men's room after a Patrick's
Day parade. Besides, you look a wreck!

Want my advice? Wag your tail and strut your stuff,
coif up your hair like a powder puff.
And for God's sake, get rid of that cough.

It's Halloween. Put on your costume, masque-
R-ade as a French poodle. With any luck,
a man in a *Burberry* mackintosh,

or a woman in *Prada* or mink
will take you home to a penthouse (*Wink! Wink!*).
Ah, then, my dear girl, you'll be in the pink.

MOSAIC
i.m. Grace Farrell

I

Hey, Mr Mosaic Man, decorate a lamppost
in her honour in your East Village basilica.
Use the finest Venetian gilded glass
and moss-green Connemara marble.
Not for her your broken bottles or shards of china.
Place her at the centre of a golden dome, draped
in lapis lazuli from the mines of Afghanistan;
flanked by moonstoned seraphim and jaded saints.
Take your time, assemble her square by square
by square, like a Chuck Close portrait.

II

Dead to the world in Alphabet City,
on a cardboard-scattered bed in a drafty
alcove of a famine church. Earlier:
panhandling on Houston, sidewalk hotdogs with
a park ally. Hooded punters and wrapped-up poets
legging it to lit-up clubs and theatres.
Now, the shelter curfew has come
and gone; the dogs from the dog run are home,
curled up in their L.L. Bean plaid doggie beds.
The irascible wind buffaloing in off the river
shakes her awake. Drawing the coarse blanket around
her whippet-thin bones, she folds her arms
into an X across her chest, pulls her frozen feet
up under her. Why she can't go home is anybody's guess.

Cigarette dangling between cracked lips, she reaches
for her Bic – *flicks, flicks, flicks* the sparkwheel
till a shivering nimbus appears. The light so bright,
she shades her eyes, releases her thumb.

But the darkness she expects fails to return,
the brick nook flush with brilliance. Standing
by the blue tubular scaffolding, a cowled woman,
a bowl of fire in one hand, an oak crozier
in the other. *Liz, is that you?* she calls
to the figure above her. *My name is Brigid,*
the woman replies, removing her woollen poncho
and placing it over the younger woman's legs.
Brace yerself, Brigid! Come in, yeh must be foundered.
She proffers a flagon to the stranger,
which she accepts.
So, on and on into the biting night
– the bottle and the butt passing back and forth –
the two women chinwag about Cork, Kildare
and Drogheda. About gospel books, Celtic knots
and what not. All the while, Brigid braiding strips
of cardboard from the floor. Dawn she takes her leave,
but not before leaving her calling card: a fylfot cross.

LIPSTICK

The kind of night when branches
beat against a bedroom window,

or an enamel bucket clangs
across a gravel yard,

a knock comes to the door.
A boy is awakened from sleep.

Muffled voices from the kitchen
(his mother's and another woman's).

Clink of spoons on saucers.
A poker stirring the embers.

Barefoot, he peers around
the kitchen door. His mother shoos him

back to bed. But not before
he's seen the dripping sickle

of blood on the woman's white china tea cup.

THE SCREAMERS

I

It was a housemother from Donegal
who told me about these free thinkers on Innisfree.
How, like a cult of squalling gulls,
they'd scream and scream, the salty winds
carrying their angst out over the Atlantic.

II

No more than six years old in my wooden cot,
I was shaken from sleep by two caterwauling girls
being beaten for smoking in the Swiss Drawer.

As thwacks and shrieks punctured the thin partition,
I could see the barrel-chested nun – tongue protruding
from the side of her mouth – threshing bare flesh with
a wooden spoon, hear her grunt from the exertion.

III

To hear my mother yawl
on the far side of the door,
but worse than that,
to hear nothing at all.

TRIMBLE'S BRIDGE

Trimble's 1797 stone bridge
straddles the hourglass canal.

On each bank, an ample grey leg
sprouts dandelions and daisies,

ochre moss-stubble on the inner thighs.
Across two centuries, the absentee landlord

hears echoes of a woman screaming.
A man on his knees forces his wife's head

under the teal water. In the shadows,
two children in wellingtons tremble.

DOCTOR RABBIT

Mother smokes Woodbines across
the blue half-door; smiles at us sitting
in the road. (Rarely does a car pass
in 1971.) My brother and I spend hours
bursting tar bubbles with twigs.

Every now and then, a hairy-molly
or a ladybird crawls up
a bare leg or arm. For sport,
we piss into jam jars behind the house
to see who pisses the most.

Mostly I win, though the hot urine
runs over my hands and soils
my knickers. A traveller woman,
a shawl about her head, a wicker basket
on her arm, comes calling.

The blessings of God on you, Missus,
would you like to buy a few clothes pegs?
Ten for thrupence, two dozen for sixpence!
Mother takes three brown-hen pennies from
the dresser; places them in the traveller's hand.

After a feed of tea, sliced pan
and butter, she sets out again
for the long road. Mother fetches
the washing from the hedges
and shakes them for earwigs. Cyclops, the dog,

smirks at Win-jims, the cat. But in the back
of our minds, we wonder if father
will come home in a good mood
or a bad one. If he'll cycle into town
or if he'll stay put.

It's Saturday and he quits work early.
His tanned muscles glisten from scything
Winstons' ditches. It's a good sign when
he whistles coming up the road.
He decides to take me blackberry picking

along the Canal Line. He smells
of Palmolive soap and Brylcream
as we saunter up the road, our enamel
buckets in tow. Past Winstons'
gravel avenue up to the Big House.

Past the well, where mother draws water
and picks watercress. Past Mrs Kirby
pruning her roses. *Joe's bringing*
the last of the turf home today.
Isn't it shocking about poor Biddy Bryant,

God between us and all harm.
We make a left at the narrow,
crooked bridge over the Grand Canal.
(Straight ahead is the road into town).
Father takes the twine from Cyclops' neck,

and the dog swims in the indolent water,
his head bobbing like a buoy. I think
of the day he tried to drown Mother
in the canal, his hand grasping her blonde mane
as he plunged her head up and down.

A mile up the mossy bank, a hanging
garden of brambles buckles with gorged spawn.
One for the bucket; two for me.
Honeyed blood drips from my lips;
black roe inks the white enamel.

In the distance, a skylark mimics
father's whistling. A butterfly
flirts with, then kisses, a wildflower.
Begob, I'd murder a pint of porter.
He doesn't turn back. We amble hand in hand

toward the bog till we reach the dump,
where father likes to rummage.
Today, among the discarded tyres
and polyethylene manure bags, he spies
a plastic doll: a rabbit with a blue tailcoat,

a stethoscope around his dirty pink neck.
Doctor Rabbit father christens him.
Later, Daddy will waltz us both around
the kitchen on his hobnail boots,
as mother, peering over her bowl of berries,

waits for the other shoe to drop.

ARE YEH THERE, MISSUS?

Are yeh there, Missus? she'd call to his wife
at unholy hours of the night,
looking for a fag or a sup of water,
never saying what really brought her
to their doorstep: the lull and hum of a warm
kitchen at day's end; the smell of baked bread
or off-the-line clothes drying by the range;
the rounded fists of a come-back-here husband.

But one winter's night she didn't call.
Next morning he found her wrapped in a shawl
of frost beneath a sheet of galvanized steel.
Fearing she might be dead, he ran from the field; fetched
a neighbour, who poked her with a stick. *God bless us,
it moved!* Carried her to his house: *Hang in there, Missus!*

RONDEAU ON HEARING OF YOUR SUICIDE

We made a home out of a stone cowshed
that summer when we were ten. Instead
of skipping rope in the orphanage yard,
we ran, sandaled and sunned, through the boulevard
of hedgerows to our home in the fields. Spread

a tablecloth for high tea (sweets we'd hid
in the wall from Saturday's pocket money).
We swept dung, pulled weeds from the floor.
We made a home.

Hung wallpaper on the lichened walls; thread-bare
curtains on imagined windows. We outdid
ourselves. Pricked our fingers with thistles; became blood
sisters. But the farmer had no regard –
kicked us off his land. He didn't care that
we made a home.

SEXUAL ABUSE: ONE

I refuse to gussy it up
in Sunday-best similes;

I will not hide it behind
a masquerade of metaphors.

Suffice to know that
all these years on

I can still hear him
tapping the head of his

soft-boiled egg with a spoon
the morning after.

I DREAMT I SAW PETER TYRRELL LAST NIGHT
to the tune of the American folk song
I Dreamed I Saw Joe Hill Last Night

I dreamt I saw Peter Tyrrell last night,
alive as he could be.
Says I, *but Pete, you're decades dead.*
I never died, says he.
I never died, says he.

The Christian Brothers killed you, Pete,
they lit the match, says I.
Takes more than straps to kill a man,
says Pete, *I didn't die.*
Says Pete, *I didn't die.*

But Scotland Yard, Pete, says I,
him looming big as Fionn,
they found your charred remains that day.
Says Pete, *I never died.*
Says Pete, *I never died.*

And standing in his tailored coat,
his back and head rod-straight,
says Pete, *what they can never kill*
went on to germinate,
went on to germinate.

From Paddy Doyle to Mannix Flynn,
in every book and air,
where courageous folk mine their past,
you're sure to find me there,
you're sure to find me there.

From Christine Buckley to Mary R.,
in every march and speech,
wherever children's shoes are hung,

it's there you'll find ould Pete.
It's there you'll find ould Pete.

I dreamt I saw Peter Tyrrell last night,
alive as he could be.
Says I, *but Pete, you're decades dead.*
I never died, says he.
I never died, says he.

THE CARDIGAN

Even the most crudely sewn initials seem to have conveyed
a special kind of intimacy, sustaining the child's individual
bond with its mother in the face of the institution.

John Styles, curator of the *Threads of Feeling* exhibition, a collection
of mid-18th century tokens left with abandoned babies at the
London Foundling Hospital

I

Monogrammed swatches snugged amid the swaddling,
tokens and talismans, identifiers
should the bottom-of-the-barrel poor
or end-of-her-tether mother return to reclaim her child.
Lockets and padlocks, topknots and cockades, a humble
hazel-nut shell swinging on a yellow ribbon.
Buttons and thimbles, poems and playing cards,
an ivory pen-knife scrimshawed with flowers.
Notched copper ha'pennies and silver sixpences,
a smooth farthing fashioned into an 'S'. Fish-shaped bone
gambling chips and crusty curled-up cauls – timeless
tokens tucked away in orphanage billet books.

II

On bone-numbing nights, my mother would place a red
lemonade bottle full of warm water at the foot
of the bed to warm my feet, throw an extra coat
on top of the bedclothes, and if there was a spare
bottle of stout in the house, pour half
a cupful for me. Hunkering by the bed,
she'd whisper, *drink it up, pet, it's good for you.*
Love's little labours not lost on me
a few years later as I wrestled with the night
in the industrial school dormitory.

After her funeral, my father gave me a child's red
Fair Isle cardigan she'd kept in a suitcase on top
of the wardrobe. It wasn't the vision of my
four-year-old self romping through the three-roomed
council house in it, little Dutch children
clog-dancing on a floor of tick-tack-toe,
a row of white buttons like lozenges,
that brought me to my knees, but my mother's
six crude mendings. Stitches like dog's teeth
fastening each sleeve, a fragment of fabric
reinforcing the bottom button, and below the elbow,
a square of woven red yarn. I picture her by the range
bent over her work, running stitches to cover
the moth-eaten hole. Years, darning and undarning.

THE OLD WOMAN WHO LIVED IN A SHOE

21 pregnancies in 25 years –
three stillborn, three miscarriages,
15 healthy babies – and one drunken husband.
She didn't know what to do.

And I, the middle child – seven older,
seven younger, seven brothers, seven sisters –
childless. Soon my eggs will shrivel.
She tells me never to have children.

But I see her stare at the fair-haired schoolboy
in the restaurant, her lithium shakes
spilling the milky tea from her plastic beaker.
That could've been her Tony before

the nuns took him. She turns to me and smiles
a gummy smile, her head bobbing like
a bobble-head dog in the rear window of a car.
I look away, ask for the bill.

Earlier, I wanted to ask her what happened
to the new shoes she promised me on a visit
to the orphanage years ago. (She wrote all our sizes
down on lined notepaper; tucked it in her handbag).

Instead, I offered to buy her a pair of shoes.
She claimed she hadn't had new shoes in
50 years of marriage. I believed her.
I'd seen her hand-me-downs, an in-law's largesse.

In the car, she recalled a neighbour helping her
give birth: *gasping for a cup of tea,*
she never asked if I had a mouth on me.
I think she thought the old bitch

was a pro at whelping her yearly litter.
Another child was born in the back seat
of a Morris Minor on a snowy night.
Years blurred, she couldn't remember which one.

When you're 40, women don't ask why
you don't have children. They offer sympathetic looks
on Mother's Day, plonk newborns in your arms
at barbeques and christenings, and if you'd let them,

tie a pair of old boots and a few tin cans
to your rear bumper as you drive away.
Passing a church, my mother blesses herself,
her moccasined feet stitched neatly together.

SEXUAL ABUSE: TWO
after Pablo Neruda

And some of you will ask why
my poetry doesn't speak
of windswept hills
or the heather on the bog
of the old sod.

Come, look at the bottle of vodka.
Come, look at the pen and paper.
Come, look at the razor blade.

Come, look, look at the razor blade.

TRANSUBSTANTIATION

As the priest held aloft the chalice at your
funeral mass, I decided to bury the past.
The earnest altar boy rang the sanctus bells –

tintinnabulum – and I bowed my head.
I forgive you, I said. *Rest in peace.*
A friend said I should expect a sign in the weeks ahead.

Miles and months away, I waited for a cardinal
or a blue jay to fly into the house.
Dusk once, a creature crept out from under

the tool shed and paused by the oak tree,
pointed his flesh-coloured snout up at the deck;
I held his sloe-eyes in mine across the years.

In the kitchen, the kettle whistled, whistled, whistled.
Neither of us prepared to play possum, he slunk into the
bed of ivy; I opened the French doors and went inside.

AT THE ALGONQUIN
for Pete

I'd buried my mother two months earlier
– as the earth delivered her bounty of bluebells
and daffodils – in the wind-licked graveyard beside

the village church she'd robbed in another lifetime.
You did your best, I wrote on the white-rose wreath,
considering ... what more can you ask of a person?

Although, I did ask her (again) as she lay
slender as a snowdrop in her hospital bed,
her white head pendent, if I should have a child.

And there we were at the Algonquin, sipping
sherry like a couple of round table aesthetes,
Matilda the cat lounging on her chaise longue in the lobby,

content to ignore us. (She has a nose for poseurs).
Earlier we'd held hands and threw back our heads
in laughter in a candle-lit carriage house on Barrow Street

– in for a penny, in for a pound.
And there we were riding the elevator
to the Thurber Suite, two Walter Mittys, willing

to yoke our fears and fantasies; go for broke.

CAMPGROUND, THE ADIRONDACKS
for Aedan

Crouched over bicycles like jockeys at Churchill Downs,
helmeted boys traverse the wooden bridge in twos
and threes. Pasty-legged fathers in baseball caps,
on the annual pilgrimage, secure feather fishing lures
on rods before casting their lot with gung-ho sons
in neon t-shirts. Around the lake, amid the pines
and the oaks, pop-ups on pick-up trucks and sleek RVs
bide their time; further back, log-cabins and cottages
with hanging baskets and Americana whirligigs.

Low-slung sun: paddle-boats slosh slosh on the black onyx
lake; kayakers windmill their way from here to there.
Mothers in inflatables catch up on books on Nooks or bask
themselves like turtles on rocks. At the water's edge, a boy
skims stones, his black lab running to and fro. And here,
an old-timer in a lawn chair, as still as Abe in DC, staring
at nothing in particular. There, a man in a sleeveless
muscle shirt flips burgers on a grill; a family plays cards
around a Gingham picnic table. Hackles relaxed,

a wife laughs at a joke her husband makes. Suspended
in air, a disco ball of midges. Higher again, a hawk
freewheels. By the front gate, a formidable woman (the
spit of Madeleine Albright) in shorts and Argyle knee-
highs directs traffic with a paddleboard: *your kid got a
helmet? Can't ride no bike 'round here without a helmet!*
Her first act as secretary of the lake.
Over by the horseshoe pits, boys pull vintage cap guns
from imaginary holsters. *Bang! Bang! You're dead!*

Close your eyes. Listen. To the barking dog; the tinging of
a distant hammer. Smell the woodsmoke. After the fishing,
the hiking and the swimming; after the trolley buses to
and from Saratoga, there'll be blazing fires and tiki-torches,

hot dogs and hamburgers, and if you're really good,
a sundae at the Pavilion. Campers will gather around fire
rings, lean in to roast marshmallows on twigs,
filling the silences with remember whens.
The lucky few will launch sky lanterns into the night.

But after the catch, comes the release: rigs with names
like *Conquest, Greyhawk and Safari* will lumber back
to the leaf blowers and the lawn worship, the strip malls
and the bumper to bumper. Back to clapboard houses with
barnstars and post-mounted mailboxes with little red flags.
Still, after the sprinklers are blown out, the bags
of leaves at the curb and the final trick-or-treater home,
let there always be the floating sky candles
carrying prayers to the summer super moon.

Epigraph:
'Keep digging for the good turf' is part of a note, written on an American Express table reservation card, from Seamus Heaney to the author in New York City, 1998, when she worked as a waitress in an Irish bar/restaurant.

On Looking Into The Sunday Press *Photo of Convent Children Looking into a Stable:*
A well-to-do farmer and his wife in the townland of Bethlehem, County Westmeath invited a busload of children from Mount Carmel Orphanage to their farm for a Christmas celebration. A nativity scene was set up in one of the stables, and the children sang hymns around the crib. It was the front-page story in *The Sunday Press,* 20 December 1970.

Inheritance:
In Seamus Heaney's poem *Station Island* (VIII), his cousin Colum McCartney accuses the poet of whitewashing ugliness in a previous poem: *[you] saccharined my death with morning dew.*
During requiem mass for the 35 children lost in the Cavan fire, the Bishop of Kilmore said, *Dear little angels, now before God in Heaven, they were taken away before the gold of their innocence had been tarnished by the soil of the world.*
This poem was inspired by the 1985 book *Children of the Poor Clares: The Story of an Irish Orphanage,* by Mavis Arnold and Heather Laskey. I did not change any of the names.
Prayer: *Litany of the Blessed Virgin Mary,* often recited after the rosary.

Letterfrack Man:
Sent at the age of eight into the care of the Christian Brothers at Letterfrack Industrial School, Galway, Peter Tyrrell, a Galway native himself, suffered appallingly from the brutality of the school's regime. As an adult, he fought, with the help of Senator Owen Sheehy Skeffington, to highlight the abuses that occurred in Irish industrial schools. An account of his time in Letterfrack and his later life was told in a series of letters to Sheehy Skeffington, which was found in the archives of the National Library of Ireland in 2003. Tyrrell tragically ended his own life in 1967 by immolating himself in a London park.

Redress cheque: The Redress Board was set up under the Residential Institutions Redress Act, 2002 in Ireland to make awards to persons who, as children, were abused while resident in industrial schools.

fruit-and-veg vendor: Tunisian uprising.

Goldenbridge, Ferryhouse, Artane: Irish industrial schools known for their harsh treatment of inmates.

The Boys From the Bunkhouse:
'The "Boys" in the Bunkhouse' is an investigative piece, written by *New York Times* reporter Dan Barry, about a few dozen men from Texas with intellectual disabilities who worked in servitude for decades in a turkey processing plant in the town of Atalissa, Iowa. It was published on 9 March 2014.

Late-night Sport:
Sassenach: An English person.
Tiocfaidh ár lá: Our day will come (Irish Republican Army slogan).

Wounds:
Cruelty Man: A moniker for the local inspector from the ISPCC, the Irish Society for the Prevention of Cruelty to Children.
Prayer: *Anima Christi,* a medieval prayer to Jesus.

Litany:
Title references the prayer *The Litany of the Saints.*

Rhesus:
Poem references American psychologist Harry Harlow's late-50s/early-60s maternal-separation experiments with rhesus monkeys.

A Modest Proposal:
Mother Catherine McAuley founded the Sisters of Mercy order of nuns in Ireland in 1831.

Lady Bracknell's Take on Misery Lit:
Misery Lit. A genre of supposedly biographical literature mostly concerned with the protagonist's triumph over personal trauma or abuse, often during childhood.
Lady Bracknell: A character in Oscar Wilde's play *The Importance of Being Earnest*. A Lady Bracknell quote: 'To lose one parent, Mr. Worthing, may be regarded as a misfortune. To lose both looks like carelessness'.

Three Sheets:
The pledge: The Pioneer Total Abstinence Association, founded in 1898, is an Irish organisation for Roman Catholic teetotalers. Its members are commonly called Pioneers. To 'take the pledge' is to abstain from alcohol.

Oasis:
Butlin's Mosney: Part of a chain of large affordable holiday camps, founded in the UK by Billy Butlin. The Irish Butlin's opened in Mosney, County Meath in 1948. At its peak, the camp could accommodate close to 3,000 campers and 4,000 day visitors. It included the trade-mark chalets, huge dining hall, amusement arcade, ballroom, swimming pools, a boating lake, and a sunken rose garden. Butlin's Redcoats is the name given to the frontline staff at Butlin's holiday camps, who wear red blazers and white pants or skirts.

Audition:
A friend adopted an eight-year-old child from a Russian orphanage. The young girl and her friends were filmed for prospective parents. This poem was inspired by Irina's video.

Sister Raphael and the Orphan Girl:
Imní: Irish word for anxiety.

Banister:
Mary Raftery: An Irish investigative journalist and filmmaker. Her documentary series, *States of Fear*, exposed decades of abuse in Irish state-sponsored, church-run industrial schools and orphanages and prompted an apology from and an investigation by the Irish government.
The poem was inspired by Mary's fond memory of climbing the stairs as a young child and falling into her father's open arms.

Seeing:
Shellagopukka: Irish slang word for snail.

Mosaic:
Grace Farrell was a 35-year-old Irish woman who froze to death in an alcove of St Brigid's Church, East Village, New York City, 19 February 2011. She came to New York at the age of 17 to study art.

When she was a child, she spent several years in a children's home in Drogheda.

Mosaic Man: Jim Power is a mosaic artist, who emigrated from Ireland to the United States in 1959. Since the 1980s he has been decorating lampposts in New York City's East Village. He is known as the *Mosaic Man.*

Liz Hooper was a 50-year-old homeless woman who died in NYC, 2011, in the same alcove of St Brigid's Church where Grace Farrell was found seven months earlier.

One of the inspirations for this poem was Hans Christian Anderson's story *The Little Match Girl.*

Brace yourself, Brigid: An Irish joke – an Irishman's idea of foreplay.

Fylfot cross: Saint Brigid's cross.

The Screamers:

The Screamers: In 1974 on the island of Innisfree, off the coast of Donegal, a group of free thinkers formed a community called the Atlantis Foundation. They earned the moniker *The Screamers* because they practiced Primal Screaming Therapy.

The Swiss Drawer: The name of one of the rooms in the orphanage which included lavatories and baths.

I Dreamt I Saw Peter Tyrrell Last Night:

Paddy Doyle, Mannix Flynn, and Christine Buckley: ex-inmates of industrial schools, and long-time campaigners against institutional abuse.

Wherever children's shoes are hung: Easter Sunday mass at the Pro Cathedral in Dublin, 2010, protesters of institutional abuse hung hundreds of children's shoes on the outside railings.

Sexual Abuse: Two:

Pablo Neruda's poem *I'm Explaining a Few Things* inspired this poem.

My profound gratitude to the Arts Council/An Chomhairle Ealaíon for a Literature Bursary which enabled me to finish this collection, and to Poetry Ireland for selecting me for their introductions series. Sincere thanks also to the Patrick Kavanagh Centre and Listowel Writers' Week. A special thank you to Dean Bernard Firestone, Dr Joseph Fichtelberg and Dr Craig Rustici, Hofstra University for their generous support, including travel bursaries. With great pleasure I thank my creative writing teachers throughout the years, who have long believed in my work and encouraged me: Susan Gubernat, Marilyn Hacker, Marie Ponsot, Molly Peacock, Phillis Levin, Janet Kaplan and Erik Brogger. I am indebted to Molly Peacock, Brian Lynch and Alan Hayes for their editorial help.

An earlier version of this manuscript won the 2010 Patrick Kavanagh Award (the manuscript was entitled *Not the Delft School*), and was awarded the 2013 Listowel Writers' Week Poetry Collection Award (the manuscript was entitled *Omphalos*). Six of these poems were published in the *Listowel Writers' Week Winners Anthology*.

Grateful acknowledgement is made to the following publications in which these poems, or earlier versions of them, first appeared:
Irish Pages: 'Not the Delft School'
The Sunday Tribune: 'On Looking into *The Sunday Press* Photo of Convent Children Looking into a Stable', 'The Cupboard'
The Irish Times: 'Omphalos', 'Arts and Crafts'
THE SHOp: 'Arts and Crafts', 'For the Love of God'
Towards Forgiveness Anthology: 'The Old Woman Who Lived in a Shoe'
Poetry Salzburg Review: 'Lipstick', 'Rhesus', 'Sexual Abuse: One', '(Eden) Derry'

The Recorder: The Journal of the American Irish Historical Society: 'Altar', 'Quiet Time', 'Earliest Memory'
The Irish Examiner, USA: 'The Laundry'
The PPA Literary Review: 'Rondeau on Hearing of Your Suicide'
The Complete Idiot's Guide to Writing Poetry: 'The Bread Bin Was Empty'
Boyne Berries: 'A Winter's Night'
North West Words: 'The Screamers', 'Pallas Lake'

'Quiet Time' was a finalist in the 2001 Strokestown International Poetry Competition.
'Omphalos' was broadcast on BBC Radio Ulster's *Arts Extra*.
'On Looking into *The Sunday Press* Photo of Convent Children Looking into a Stable' and 'The Cupboard' were nominated for the 2008 Hennessy X.O. Literary Awards.
'Litany' won the 2010 Dromineer Literary Festival Poetry Competition.
'The Cardigan' received a Highly Commended Award in the 2013 iYeats Competition.
'Oasis' received a Highly Commended Award in the 2014 iYeats Competition.
'Inheritance' was shortlisted for the 2013 Fermoy International Poetry Competition.
'The Potato Picker and the TV Rental Man' was shortlisted for the 2014 Allingham Arts Festival Poetry Competition.
'Wounds' was shortlisted for the Over the Edge New Writer of the Year Award, 2014.
'Seeing' won the 2014 Boyle Arts Festival Poetry Competition.
'Banister' was published on The Mary Raftery Journalism Fund website and on the back of their annual report, 2013.

A huge thank you to my biggest fan, my sister Rita.
My brother Tony: you were with me from the beginning.
Aedan, my little man. I am so blessed to be your mother. I love you.
Pete, we're still here. You are my rock. I love you.

ABOUT THE AUTHOR

Connie Roberts, a County Offaly native, emigrated from Ireland to the United States in 1983. In 2010 she received the Patrick Kavanagh Award, was awarded first prize in the Dromineer Literary Festival poetry competition and was selected for the Poetry Ireland introductions series. In 2011 she received a Literature Bursary from the Irish Arts Council, and was nominated for the Hennessy Literary Awards. She has been a finalist in several poetry contests, including the Strokestown International Poetry Competition, the iYeats Poetry Competition (twice), the Allingham Arts Festival Poetry Competition, the Over the Edge New Writer of the Year Award, the North West Words Poetry Prize (twice), the Fermoy International Poetry Competition, the Swift Satire Contest and the Dana Awards. In 2013 Connie was awarded the Poetry Collection Award at Listowel Writers' Week and in 2014 she won the Boyle Arts Festival poetry competition. She teaches creative writing at Hofstra University, New York.